ISBN 978-0-259-50535-8
PIBN 10820343

1 MONTH OF
FREE
READING

at

www.ForgottenBooks.com

By purchasing this book you are eligible for one month membership to ForgottenBooks.com, giving you unlimited access to our entire collection of over 1,000,000 titles via our web site and mobile apps.

To claim your free month visit:
www.forgottenbooks.com/free820343

English
Français
Deutsche
Italiano
Español
Português

www.forgottenbooks.com

Mythology Photography **Fiction**
Fishing Christianity **Art** Cooking
Essays Buddhism Freemasonry
Medicine **Biology** Music **Ancient
Egypt** Evolution Carpentry Physics
Dance Geology **Mathematics** Fitness
Shakespeare **Folklore** Yoga Marketing
Confidence Immortality Biographies
Poetry **Psychology** Witchcraft
Electronics Chemistry History **Law**
Accounting **Philosophy** Anthropology
Alchemy Drama Quantum Mechanics
Atheism Sexual Health **Ancient History**
Entrepreneurship Languages Sport
Paleontology Needlework Islam
Metaphysics Investment Archaeology
Parenting Statistics Criminology
Motivational

IMAGE EVALUATION
TEST TARGET (MT-3)

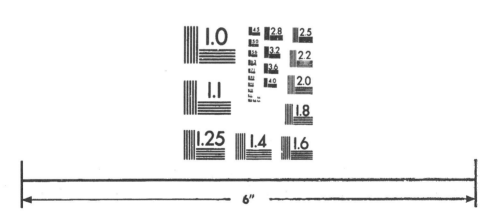

6"

CIHM/ICMH
Microfiche
Series.

CIHM/ICMH
Collection de
microfiches.

dian Institute for Historical Microreproductions / Institut canadien de microreproductions historiq

The Institute has attempted to obtain the best original copy available for filming. Features of this copy which may be bibliographically unique, which may alter any of the images in the reproduction, or which may significantly change the usual method of filming, are checked below.

L'Institut a microfilmé le me qu'il lui a été possible de se de cet exemplaire qui sont p point de vue bibliographique une image reproduite, ou qu modification dans la méthoc sont indiqués ci-dessous.

☐ Coloured covers/
Couverture de couleur

☐ Covers damaged/
Couverture endommagée

☐ Covers restored and/or laminated/
Couverture restaurée et/ou pelliculée

☐ Cover title missing/
Le titre de couverture manque

☐ Coloured maps/
Cartes géographiques en couleur

☐ Coloured ink (i.e. other than blue or black)/
Encre de couleur (i.e. autre que bleue ou noire)

☐ Coloured plates and/or illustrations/
Planches et/ou illustrations en couleur

☐ Bound with other material/
Relié avec d'autres documents

☐ Tight binding may cause shadows or distortion along interior margin/
La reliure serrée peut causer de l'ombre ou de la distortion le long de la marge intérieure

☐ Blank leaves added during restoration may appear within the text. Whenever possible, these have been omitted from filming/
Il se peut que certaines pages blanches ajoutées lors d'une restauration apparaissent dans le texte, mais, lorsque cela était possible, ces pages n'ont pas été filmées.

☐ Additional comments:/
Commentaires supplémentaires:

☐ Coloured pages/
Pages de couleur

☐ Pages damaged/
Pages endommagées

☐ Pages restored and/or
Pages restaurées et/ou

☑ Pages discoloured, stai
Pages décolorées, tach

☐ Pages detached/
Pages détachées

☑ Showthrough/
Transparence

☐ Quality of print varies/
Qualité inégale de l'im

☐ Includes supplementar
Comprend du matériel

☐ Only edition available/
Seule édition disponibl

☐ Pages wholly or partial slips, tissues, etc., hav ensure the best possibl
Les pages totalement o obscurcies par un feuill etc., ont été filmées à obtenir la meilleure im

This item is filmed at the reduction ratio checked below/

DR. COLENSO

AND THE

PENTATEUCH.

———◆———

TORONTO:

ROLLO AND ADAM, KING STREET.

LONDON:

GEORGE MORRISH, 24, WARWICK LANE, PATERNOSTER ROW.

1863.

TORONTO:
LOVELL AND GIBSON, PRINTERS, YONGE STREET.

DR. COLENSO

AND THE

PENTATEUCH.

———

I thank thee, O Father, Lord of Heaven and Earth, because thou hast hid these things from the wise and prudent and has revealed them unto babes.—MATT. XI. 25.

IT is impossible to treat the author of this book as a Christian. I do not say this as forming any judgment of his personal state, in any way; I speak of the public profession of a religion he belongs to—Chri·tianity as contrasted with heathenism, Mohammedanism, Judaism, or Buddhism. Dr. Colenso states that " our belief in the living God remains as sure as ever, though not the Pentateuch only but the whole Bible were removed. It is written on our hearts by God's own finger as surely as by the hand of the apostle in the Bible, that ' God is, and is a rewarder of them that diligently seek Him.' It is written there also as plainly as in the Bible, that ' God is not mocked,—that whatsoever a man soweth that shall he also reap,' and that ' he that soweth to the flesh shall of the flesh reap corruption,'" pp. 53, 54. That is, with the Bible or without the Bible, Dr. C. believes in the existence of God, and His rewarding them that seek Him, and in natural conscience. In other words (as far as his book goes, which he puts forth as a manifesto), he is a professed Deist. Even with the Bible he only believes so much as his heart and conscience recognize, and that the latter is to be preferred to the Bible as the means of knowing God : " that He Himself, the living God, our

Father and Friend, is nearer and closer to us than any book can be; that His voice within the heart may be heard continually by the obedient child that listens for it, and *that* shall be our teacher and guide in the path of duty, which is the path of life, when all other helpers— even the words of the best of books—may fail us," p. 54. Now it is clear that neither believing that God is, nor natural conscience, is believing in the special facts of Christianity—the incarnation, atonement, resurrection, redemption, being born again, the exaltation of a man to God's right hand, the Father, Son, and Holy Ghost. In a word, no special truth or *fact* of Christianity is "written on our hearts by God's own finger," or can be possessed by mere natural conscience or belief in God. All *intervention* of God is left out. But it is in this, and the statement of what led to its necessity, that revealed religion consists. There *is* a conscience in every man. The word of God acts on it. I do not doubt that there is an instinctive knowledge of a God and of judgment. This is all **Dr. C.** owns, with or without the Bible. Revealed religion is a series of divine and marvellous facts and truths, unfolding an intervention of God in grace with sinful man. He sets this aside. His relation-ship with God is not founded on it. He prefers, as teaching, what he has without it; that is, he wholly and professedly sets aside Christianity. He goes farther—he recognizes " the voice of God's Spirit . . . . not in the Bible only, but out of the Bible : not to us Christians only, but to our fellow-men of all climes and countries, ages and religions, the same gracious Teacher is reveal-ing, in different measures, according to His own good pleasure, the hidden things of God," p. 222. Dr. C. has, in substance, solemnly declared that this is not so (see Article xviii. of the Thirty-nine Articles) ; but I suppose this is no matter with rationalists. But his statement amounts to this : Christians and heathens have all their particular religions, but beside and within this, all have a communication in their own hearts of the hidden things of God. The knowledge of God is not in the religion, for heathens and Christians have it more or less, whatever their religion, in their hearts. He confirms this by quotations from Cicero, Sikhs and Hindoos. Cicero's statement—I suppose Dr. C. did not find it out—is merely asserting natural conscience, with the addition of a denial of the foundation fact of revelation, that man is a sinner, driven out from God. " Whoever will not obey this law," says Cicero, " will be flying from himself, and having treated with contempt his human nature will, in that very fact, pay the greatest penalty, even if he shall have escaped other punishments, as they are commonly considered." Now this makes human nature the measure of good, as indeed Cicero everywhere does. And just see the result, which neither Dr. C. nor Lactantius, from whom he quotes, seem to have noticed : this law or right reason " to the good never commands or forbids in vain, never influences the wicked either by commanding or forbidding." Could grace be more fully denied ? Could the effect of law or conscience be more entirely misstated ? There are good or wicked already—God knows how—and this law or right reason changes nothing,— always succeeds with one, and leaves the other where he is. This is, we are told, " a voice almost divine." " The same divine Teacher revealed also to the Sikh Gooroos (teachers) such great truths as these," p. 223. He then quotes statements of the unity of God, but which is Pantheism, that is, that God is in every thing ; statements which recognize Mahomets, Brahmas, Vishnus, Sivas—of course *not* Christ—and that is a revelation of God for Dr. C. He then quotes from Hindoo writings " the following words, which were written by one who had no Penteteuch nor Bible to teach him, but who surely learned such living truths as these by the direct teaching of the Spirit of

God," p. 224. In these words God is celebrated, and
there is a good deal of moralizing, such as may be found
anywhere; but in which we find, " He that partaketh of
but one grain of the love of God shall be released from
the sinfulness of all his doubts and actions "--a comfort.
able quietus. " I take for my spiritual food the water
and the leaf of Ram." " God dwelleth in the mind, and
none other but God." Dr. C. admires what is the avowed
doctrine of these same teachers, without finding out it is
the grossest folly of Pantheism. " God is the gift of
charity, God is the offering, God is the fire of the altar,
by God the sacrifice is performed, and God is to be ob.
tained by him who makes God alone the object of his
work." Everything being but a development or expan.
sion of God, we are too, and, of course, so far as we
realize God in it, become God in a superior degree. But
all is God; and it is true of all things, man among the
the rest. This last sentence, as Dr. C. approvingly quotes,
was by " one who had experienced somewhat of what
Job had experienced," p. 223. All this is but extracting
Deism from Christianity and heathenism alike, and making conscience the judge of what is to be received from
each; only, unfortunately, Dr. C.'s conscience accepts
the very grossest Pantheism without so much as finding
it out.

But there is more than this. This book does not believe as much of Christ as Mohammed did. Dr. C. openly
professes to know much better than Christ upon the subject of the divine authority of revelation. Mohammed held
Christ to be a prophet, and that He will judge the world.
On the last point the book does not declare itself, if it be
not in an intimation borrowed from Cicero. Here is Dr.
C.'s estimate of Christ's authority in what he declared:
" We are expressly told, in Luke ii. 52, that Jesus increased in *wisdom* as well as in stature. It is not supposed that in His human nature He was acquainted, more

than any educated Jew of the age, with the mysteries of all modern sciences, nor, with St. Luke's expressions before us, can it be seriously maintained that, as an *infant* or *young child* He possessed a knowledge surpassing that of the most pious and learned adults of His nation, upon the subject of the authority and age of the different portions of the Pentateuch. At what period, then, of His life upon earth, is it to be supposed that He had granted to Him, as the Son of man, *supernaturally*, full and accurate information on these points, so that He should be expected to speak about the Pentateuch in other terms than any other devout Jew of that day would have employed? Why sho'' '' '' be ''hought that He would speak with certain *divin* :dge on this matter more than upon other matter .ry science or history?" p. 32. That is, when Cbri: :ed One, spoke of the authority of the Word of God, : authoritatively of the Scriptures and of Moses,—He merely followed the ignorance and prejudice of the pious Rabbis of his nation. Dr. Colenso has more knowledge, and is freed from the prejudices, and in consequence can tell us positively that Christ was wrong! He has found out that it is impossible that such things as are found in the Pentateuch could come from our loving Father. This, if we are to believe Dr. C., Christ had not moral discernment enough to find out, and took for granted all was right, so as to believe that what Moses wrote came from God. Now Christ says, " We speak that we do know, and testify that we have seen," for He was of and in heaven; and the question is not how He learned what He knew but, when He taught positively, did He teach perfectly, or only under the influence of national prejudice? Dr. C. quotes the following passages of Christ's words:—" Had ye believed Moses ye would have believed me, for he wrote of me; but if ye believe not his writings how shall ye believe my words." But it seems this appeal was all beside the mark, for Moses never wrote it at all. Hence, of course, they were not called upon to believe Christ's words either. " Now that the dead are raised, even Moses shewed at the bush." This too was quite a mistake. " They have Moses and the prophets, let them hear them. If they hear not Moses and the prophets, neither will they be per- suaded though one rose from the dead." But all this solemn appeal of Christ to Moses, as of equal authority and weight with His own words and resurrection, as a proof of truth, is a mistake, the prejudice of pious Rabbis of His nation ! Dr. C. is freed from them, and can prove he knows much better than Christ did. And this man is what is called " Bishop of Natal." I may be asked, has he not declared his belief in all the canonical Scriptures, and bound himself in this office to require it of those he ordains ? He has. What then does he do with his conscience ? He tells us that too : it is governed by the Court of Arches. It is a mercy for upright men that modern rationalists shew themselves so plainly morally. I do not think I ever read any thing so morally base as the reasons for signing the Articles, in the " Essays and Reviews." Old infidels broke with Christianity—it was sad enough—but modern ones keep their places and only give up their faith.

The boldness of Dr. C.'s assertions, and the excessive carelessness of his statements and conclusions, are alike remarkable. He tells us that he does not believe in the deluge, because he does in geology. He has studied it in the Zulu country, and he now knows for certain (for Sir C. Lyell is infallible, if Scripture and the Lord Christ be not) that a universal deluge could not possibly have taken place. Now Sir C. Lyell is unquestionably an able geo- logist, as well as the constant resort and refuge of infi- dels ; but he has a system, and a system which geologists less speculative and, at the very least, as able as he, en- tirely reject. Nor does he deny that the science is in its infancy. The ablest inquirers believe in a universal deluge; the latest researches tend to prove it. I say tend, because no certain conclusions can yet be made from geology as to dates. I do not hesitate to affirm, and I am supported by the ablest geologists, that geological dates and periods stand on the most uncertain and unsatisfactory footing. Sir C. Lyell's system is utterly unsatisfactory,—irreconcileable with the evident facts of the upheaval theory, which is generally admitted. Dr. C. assures us that a partial deluge is no better, so that in spite of universal tradition, Script．..., the authority of Christ, who refers specifically to the deluge as true (Matt. xxiv. 37–39), and much geological research, we are to have no deluge at all. 'I do not know that I should ever have noticed this point, as it is impossible to follow it out here, but as affording a proof of Dr. C.'s manner of reasoning. It was not partial, he says, because a flood which should cover Ararat must, in due time, sweep over the Puy de Dôme, because water finds its own level!—that is to say, water 16,000 or 17,000 feet deep in a narrow locality must have been some 5,000 feet deep at thousands of miles' distance, when it had spread that distance in every direction! And a man who reasons thus is to call in question the accuracy of Scripture. But Dr. Colenso assures us the Scriptures never affirm their own infallibility. Abstractedly " infallibility " belongs to a person, not to what has been already said; but they affirm that they are inspired by God, and that they have His authority. The Lord says, " The Scripture cannot be broken "—appeals to it, as we have seen, as of equal authority with His own words—refers to them as testifying of Him—expounds them after His resurrection in what they taught concerning Himself—declares that all they said must be fulfilled—opens His disciples' understanding to understand them—declares that His rising from the dead would be useless to convince those by whom they

were not believed ;—they are quoted by Him as absolutely conclusive authority. Facts here questioned, or
borne with because they may be " fairly disposed of,"
are referred to by Christ as undoubted history. So the
apostles write whole epistles, in which their entire
teaching is based upon the truth and inspired authority
of Scripture. Paul speaks of the Scriptures " foreseeing,"
so completely does he identify them with God. " But
what saith the Scripture" is conclusive : not only so—
they declare them to be by inspiration. They are called
the oracles of God, and the possession of them is counted
to be the main privilege of God's people ; so the law is
called " the living oracles." Peter says, " No prophesy
of the Scripture is of any private interpretation, but holy
men of God spake as they were moved by the Holy Ghost."
I dare say Dr. C. will call the authenticity of this in question. Take, then, the first Epistle (though I am perfectly
satisfied of the authenticity of the second). There he
states that the prophets searched as men into their own
prophecies, as given by the Spirit of Christ which was
in them. Paul declares that " Every Scripture is given
by inspiration of God "—the security of the saint in the last
perilous times. He calls the Scriptures " prophetic Scriptures" (Scriptures of the prophets). I have no doubt
this refers to the New Testament, but if it be the Old, it is
saying they are inspired. So his own teaching he declares to be by " words which the Holy Ghost teacheth."
The prophets were infamous impostors, if what they said
were not the direct testimony of God himself, for they
say, " Thus saith the Lord." As to Christ, it is said,
" He whom God hath sent speaketh the words of God, for
God giveth not the Spirit by measure unto Him." Thus,
as Son of man, what He spoke He spoke—to refer to
Dr. C.'s question—" supernaturally," and His words were
the words of God. I am aware that Dr. C. says that, on
such subjects, He was no wiser than other pious Jews, and

that he thinks himself wiser than Christ and the apostles on such ; but does he expect every one to have the same opinion of him that he has of himself? Does he think that many even will respect the judgment of one called a Bishop, who persuades us that Christ was prejudiced and *he* is not? Poor human nature !

Allow me to ask yóu, Dr. Colenso, do you believe in the resurrection? do you believe in this stupendous exercise of Divine power, so suited to man subject to death? I mean the resurrection of him who was " delivered for our offences and raised again for our justification." Is it not something, this coming in of God to take out of death and from among the dead His own Son, given for our sins? Do you find this without a revelation? Does Cicero furnish you with this, or do Sikh Gooroos, or Pantheistic Brahmins? They may say fine things about God and patience, and do the same things (as Paul says) as the rest : can they tell of the deliverance of sinful man? I can conceive no greater proof of imbecility and wilful ignorance of facts than to compare the revelation first of the whole history of man, under God's dealings with his responsibility, and then of atonement and the intervention of God in deliverance, with the fine sayings of some heathen,—one who shows, too, men to be incapable of knowing God, as Cicero does, or with the moralizing of Pantheists.

But I close. I am not writing a book on these things, but penning an ephemeral article on the poorest piece of infidelity I ever met with, and I turn to the objections to run them over rapidly. Let my reader only remember this. The object of Scripture is not to meet objections or give history, but, on the part of God, what is divinely instructive to man ; that, if the Old Testament gave the perfection of the New,—it would prove it was not true, for the true light did not shine till Christ came ; that, meeting objections does not give the force of the positive

proofs. It seems candid to quote Kurtz and Hengsten-
berg (men who, however respectable, know little, as I
judge, of the power of Scripture), but in merely giving an-
swers to objections all the positive proofs are, of course,
left out. If no answer could be given to an objection,
and yet there were positive proof of that against which
the objection was brought, this would only prove the so-
lution of the difficulty was not known. The positive
proofs of the truth of Scripture are such, that the denial of
their being, as they are called, " the oracles of God " is
an evidence only of the moral darkness of the rejector of
them. It is quite true I cannot explain light to a blind
man; but every one who sees knows he *is* blind. Above
all, let my reader remember that the Lord himself treats the
Scriptures as absolutely inspired and authoritative, quotes
them as we now have them, and declares that all written
of Him must be fulfilled,—that " not a jot or tittle can
pass from the law till all be fulfilled," the law which
Dr. C. pronounces he could not attribute to God, save as
he selects bits according to his own fancy, for he has, of
course, a perfect judgment ;—a man who sees nothing in
the minutiæ of the law, which (while a yoke in the
letter) as a shadow of good things to come, is full of the
deepest instruction : let him remember that Dr. C. presents himself as wiser and better informed than Christ,
and if he have faith to do it, pray for one who can think
so, and publish a book to tell the world he does.

Such views, they tell us, will unite all pious people in
one mother church ; and if such questions should disturb
men's minds, and a serious person would ponder and
weigh them before doing so, he has only to remember
that Dr. C. has such a sense of the petty importance of
his own position, that he cannot have leisure (so he tells
us) to ponder a while before he gives forth, pretending to
be wiser than Christ,—opinions which contradict what
Christ says.

THE first objection is that in Genesis xlvi., Hezron
and Hamul are stated to have gone down to Egypt, and
consequently to have been born in Canaan, but that this
is impossible if the ages of Judah and Joseph be considered. It is contended that Judah was forty-two when
Jacob went down into Egypt, inasmuch as Joseph was
thirty-nine. Gen. xxx. 24-26, and xxxi. 41, are cited to
prove that Joseph was born in the seventh, Judah in the
fourth year " of Jacob's double marriage." The impos-
sibility of Hezron and Hamul's going down to Egypt,
arises from this, that Judah was twenty when Joseph went
down into Egypt, and that Hezron and Hamul, who rank
in point of time with Judah's great grand children though
his own grand children by Tamar, could not have been
born when he was forty-two, i. e. twenty-two years afterwards. On the other hand it is insisted that the narra-
tive of Jacob's going down, makes sixty-six souls go
with him, and there are not sixty-six without Hezron
and Hamul.

There is no ground for the objection at all. I do not
insist on the uncertainty of the exact difference between
the ages of Judah and Joseph, as what might be added,
even if just, would hardly clear up the point; though,
bringing it perhaps within the limits of possibility, it is
sufficient to throw doubt upon Dr. C.'s assertions. But
Gen. xlvi., is simply to record the immediate descendants
of Jacob who were associated with himself in Egypt, to
give his family. Thus Er and Onan are noticed, only it is
added, they died in Canaan. It is then added " and the
sons of Pharez were Hezron and Hamul." This 12th
verse is distinctly genealogy, not that all went down
into Egypt who are named in it : for Er and Onan are

named because they are sons, while it is expressly stated they did not go down at all.*

In the 12th verse the introduction of " were " is em- phatic, and the phrase, I apprehend, clearly intended to be supplementary. It is not " Er, and Onan, and Shelah, and Pharez, and Zarah, and the sons of Pharez, Hezron, and Hamul," which would clearly have been the case if they had been goers down into Egypt. But the histo- rian stops at Zarah, and adds supplementary information : Er and Onan were on the list of sons, but they did not go down, they died before, and Pharez's sons were Hez- ron and Hamul. They are looked at as filling up the breach, but the latter half of the verse is, in contrast with going down, an explanation of the history of that fami- ly. As if he had said : these were Judah's sons, but I must add this explanation to the statement: Er and Onan never got down, for they died, and Pharez had two sons who are counted in to supply their place. For, though the leading thought be the going down of the family into Egypt, yet in order to this he gives the whole family ; and that this is so is evident, for he introduces Joseph's sons, adding they were born in Egypt. Indeed, I think it very questionable whether all Benjamin's sons were born when he came into Egypt. It was after Joseph's birth that Jacob agreed with Laban to stay longer, and staid six years. He then journeyed to Palestine, when

---

*The computation in the passage is not very clear. If we count in Er and Onan, we have thirty-three sons and grandsons. If we leave them out we must count Jacob among the souls of his own sons and daughters. However, I am disposed to include Dinah and Jacob, and leave out Er and Onan, and read thus; "These be the sons of Leah which she bare unto Jacob in Padan Aram, with his daughter Dinah, all the souls of his sons and daughters: thirty and three." As if he had said, this makes thirty and three. If not, we must count in Er and Onan, and make it mere genealogical computation of sons, and the 26th verse would be general, the computation already given excluding Jacob, and Joseph and his sons.

Joseph must have been seven years old. He was sold into Egypt at seventeen. Hence Jacob had been only ten years in Canaan when Joseph went there. Jacob had settled first at Succoth, then near Shechem, and Dinah, who was probably nearly of Joseph's age, was old enough to be ill-treated by Hamor, before Benjamin was born. For Jacob went off to Bethel after the destruction of the men of Shechem, and after leaving Bethel, Benjamin was born and Rachel died. He does not appear either in the history. Joseph is a boy, the son of Jacob's old age. Benjamin could only have been two or three years old when Joseph went down ; for if Dinah were seven or eight years old when she came to Canaan, say she was fifteen or sixteen when Hamor wronged her; seven or eight years had elapsed in Canaan before Benjamin was born, and two or three years more elapsed before Joseph went down. We must add twenty-two for the interval between Joseph's and Jacob's going down. Benjamin was thus at the utmost twenty-four or twenty-five. So he is called a " lad " (nahar) xliii. 3, and a little one (katan) in xliv. 20, and (nahar) again, 31. This being so, and giving the fullest possible age of twenty-five, which, with the three terms, is very improbable, it is very little likely that he had ten sons born to him. I doubt even whether Reuben's sons were all born, as he says, "slay my two sons." On the whole, I think it is evident that this is a genealogical list, without reference to the place of birth :—the statement of the whole family, *as* a family, who went down. This manner of giving a genealogy complete, and a general fact which is not accurately true as to each individual in it, though it characterizes the subject of recital, we have other examples of. To go no further than chapter 35 : All Jacob's sons are given, including Benjamin, immediately after the account of Benjamin's birth in Canaan, and it is added, " these are the sons of Jacob which were born to him in *Padan Aram.*" The exact genealogy was the important thing, and it is given accurately. The main fact which characterized the family was their birth away from the land of promise, in the country where Jacob served for a wife. It was no object to except Benjamin in the statement; it *was* to give the accurate history of his birth. I doubt not a moment he is a special type of Christ in connection with Israel: the son of his mother's affliction, but of his father's right hand. But it could be no *mistake* for the writer, or compiler, or whatever he was, had given all the details of his birth immediately before, and speaks in the passage itself of Jacob's being in that land. But, Benjamin being born, the time was come to give the whole family. The subjects are given with divine purpose, in view of after dealings of God, which He foreknew, not as mere histories to amuse; and hence we get distinct subjects without arrangement of dates. Dr. C. states that Judah's misconduct was after Joseph's going down to Egypt, because it is said, " at that time." Now Judah's genealogy and ways were all important because our Lord was to spring out of Judah. But after this history of Judah which lasts some twenty years at any rate, the history of Joseph's going down into Egypt is resumed where it left off. Judah's history is introduced as a separate subject parenthetically. The last verse of xxxvii., and the first verse of xxxix, are connected, and the history of Judah comes in between as a whole of twenty years by itself " At that time " is only the general epoch, and the whole history is given together. This is exceedingly common in Scripture. But as Joseph was a remarkable type of Christ, so Judah was his progenitor according to the flesh. And this Pharez and his son Hezron were so. I must add that the relative ages of Judah and Joseph are anything but clearly proved. The relative dates of Joseph's birth and his going down into Egypt, and of each to other events are far more distinctly given.

Cn the whole the purpose of the statement in Gen. xlvi., is clearly to give Jacob's family, and hence some are noticed who did not go down to Egypt, and Hezron and Hamul are specially introduced into the verse not with the list of sons, but as associated with them. The saying, " Thy father went down into Egypt threescore and ten persons, and now ye are as the stars," takes up the general fact, to shew the marvellous increase. The same is the ca.' in the New Testament, specially in Luke.

Dr. C. in fact admits the whole case where he says, " wishing to sum up the seventy souls under one category, he uses (inaccurately as he himself admits) the same expression, ' came into Egypt.' " Now this settles the whole question. He gives a category of persons, that category being Jacob's family with the general fact of that family's leaving Canaan and going into Egypt. But he introduces some who did not literally go down, though they were there. If this be so, and it is perfectly evident, Dr. C.'s argument is simply worth nothing at all. When he says : " all the souls which came into Egypt were threescore and ten," we have the demonstration that some at least who were born in Egypt, provided they were of the family that came, are accounted as coming. The case of Hezron and Hamul is much clearer, because there is only an accessory statement in the genealogy ; " and the sons of Pharez were Hezron and Hamul." And we have no need to say again with Dr. C., " the description is, of course, literally incorrect, but the writer's meaning is obvious enough," for it is literally correct, and the meaning obvious too. But I may add Dr. C.'s own remark, which shews the utter wilfulness and equal absurdity of his objection : " He wishes to specify all those out of the sons of Jacob who were living at the

B

time of the commencement of the sojourn of the Israelites in Egypt, and from whom such a multitude had
sprung at the time of the Exodus." How soon Hezron
and Hamul were born we cannot say. They are
brought into the list in connection with the loss of two of
the sons of Judah, with whose history they were connected,—one of them being ancestor of David and of
the Christ.

The next objection is really almost too absurd to notice,
but worthy the futility of rationalist arguments. Dr. C.
makes a computation of how far files of men as many
in number as could stand in front of the breadth
of the tabernacle would reach. Does he think the
writer did not know, as well as Dr. C., that all the congregation could not have stood in the court. But he was
not so morally dull as to think of it. Supposing the riot
act read to a crowd of 100,000 persons, and I say, the
riot act was read to the multitude who stood before the
magistrate, and I computed how far 100,000 men would
reach, standing in a file directly before the magistrate.
What would any one think of the sense of the person
who made the remark? Or are the crowd not responsible because they cannot hear it? Away with such
childish trifling. But the fact is there is no ground for
the remark at all. " Before the door of the tabernacle
of the congregation," has a most important meaning in
these ordinances. *Within* the tabernacle and holiest of
all was the place of Jehovah's communing directly with
Moses ; *outside*, yet in connection with the tabernacle,
the place of meeting the people, of God's going out, not in
the revelation of Himself, but in communications from
Himself to the people, and of the access of the people to
Him. All the court of the tabernacle of the congregation
was held to have this character of " before the door of
the tabernacle," and all done there and communicated
thence was done before the door of the tabernacle of the

congregation. All brought up to the court was before the door. Thus if all the people had been outside the court and Moses had stood in the doorway of the court, they would have been before the door of the tabernacle of the congregation." It was the general expression for coming up to the court or entering it, though not going near the tabernacle where the door literally was "The women," we read, "assembled themselves in troops at the door of the tabernacle of the congregation." They did not come when the tabernacle was set up in order, in troops, between the laver and the holy place. But we have the matter definitely stated.— In Exodus xl. we find, ver. 29, "he put the altar of the burnt offering by the door of the tabernacle of the congregation. . . . and he set the laver between the tent of the congregation and the altar." Thus the altar of burnt offering, the first thing met with on entering the court was by the door of the tabernacle. Now this was the place where God was to meet the children of Israel, as contrasted with meeting Moses within the veil. Exod. xxix. 42, "a continual burnt offering . . . at the door of the tabernacle of the congregation before the Lord, where I will meet you to speak there unto thee. And there I will meet with the Children of Israel." Thus Moses standing under the hangings of the cɔ ..t and speaking to the crowd without was speaking to them gathered before the door of the tabernacle. Had they been inside the court he would have turned his back to them. So when a person offered a burnt offering, he offered it at the door of the tabernacle of the congregation before the Lord.— He killed the bullock before the Lord, and the blood was sprinkled upon the altar that is by the door of the tabernacle of the congregation. They came up to the Lord there, instead of offering it where they pleased, away from him. And this was carefully secured by ordinance, as a guard against idolatry. They had to bring all the beasts they slew up before the Lord : Lev. xvii. 4. The gathering of the congregation to the door of the tabernacle was bringing them up to the court, so that Moses standing there might address them. And the place specifically pointed out for this was not at the door, but where the altar was, i. e. next the entrance of the court where the people were to come up with their sacrifices, and the Lord met with them.

Such objections as these are child's play, proving only entire ignorance of God's ways with Israel, and the purport of the ordinances, carelessness of research into them, with the pretension, the common accompaniment of ignorance, to see clearer than others, and the desire to make difficulties in presence of all the divine light which is found in what is objected to. Dr. C. seeks to prove his candour and care by showing that the elders of Israel were not all the congregation. He might have spared himself the trouble. And he has gone through sums of arithmetic to prove the size of the court. I really have not examined whether his multiplication is correct. I can suppose it.

His next objection is as to how Moses and Joshua addressed all Israel ; and he wisely informs us that the crying of the children, whose mothers must be supposed to have pushed to the first place, would hinder all but those close by from hearing. Was ever anything more childish ! Supposing all did not hear, which may very well be believed, they were all put under the responsibility of what was addressed to them, of which those who were in earnest could easily put themse'ves in possession. Supposing the elders or heads of 's were nearest, as is probable, they would have both in ained and led the others according to what was said.

The next objection is to the possibility, with so few priests, of having the bullock for a sin offering burned without the camp. Now I admit fully that the great ob-

.ject here is doctrinal not historical. There is no history at all. What is ordained was only to be done in the case of the priest's, or the whole congregation's sinning; ought never to have happened, and may never have happened. And from the way they went on (for they never circumcised ' their children, and certainly fell into idolatry) if the case did arise, they probably neglected the prescribed sacrifice. If it did happen once or twice, such a provision was no difficulty. That once or twice in forty years or even in one year, such a toilsome ceremony should mark their sin was most appropriate. Nor do I doubt a moment that though the priest was responsible and must have had and seen it done the Levites or younger priests might share the manual toil. And this is implied in the form of the Hebrew verb which is the Hiphil, " to cause to go forth ;" used no doubt consequently for " bringing forth," but which may be by another as by oneself, as it is used for causing an evil report to come on some one.*— For the rest, a walk of a mile and a half or three miles for their common bodily wants was nothing out of the way for a people who had nothing to do except to tend their cattle, which would in itself have taken them there. To suppose they used fuel as in London is simple non- .:- sense. And they chose places where wells were, and God clave the rock when there was no water. It is real-

---

* Yatsa is to go forth, as Bo is to go in or to. And hence the causative is used for bringing forth, because one who does does cause to go or come forth. But there is no ground at all for confining it to the personal act of the person causing it to come forth. Thus, not only in the case of an evil report, Hotze Dibba, cited in the text. Deut. xvi. 23, Bringing forth the tithe. Lev. xxiv. 14, Bringing forth him that had cursed. Zech. iv. 7, Gen. xxxiv. 24, 25, Bringing forth Tamar. Ex. iii. 10, Moses is to bring forth Israel from Egypt; that is, cause them to come out. So Ex. xiv. 13, Heb. 14. So in Ezra i. 8. We have those did Cyrus bring forth by the hand of Mithredath. Where he expressly uses another to have them brought out. In a word, there is no ground at all for Dr. C.'s remarks.

ly absurd bringing forward such objections. Had **Dr. C.**
been a soldier, or lived in the dirt **I** have had to live **in, he**
would have known that a walk a mile and a half out **of**
a city, for the necessities of life, was a very natural thing.

The fifth objection is first that the shekel is called **the**
shekel of the sanctuary before there was a sanctuary; **and**
that the money of which the silver sockets, &c., were made
was the redemption money, and that the census which ascertained the number of the people on which the redemption money was paid was six months afterwards, **by**
which time the number must have increased. This **has**
no foundation whatever. As to the remark that it **was**
called the shekel of the sanctuary before the sanctuary
was set up. The book is a history and gives the sum taken according to the value of the money known *when it*
was written. They paid at the time what was known,
when the book was written, as the shekel of the sanctuary, perhaps settled at the very time. As regards the numbering, it is clear the computation of the sum that was
paid is made from the numbering itself, the result **of**
which was known when the account of it was written.—
There is no *continuing* of the same number;—Exodus
xxxviii. 26, Numb. i. 46,—it is the number itself. **I**
do not know what the ground for saying six months is.
The tabernacle was set up on the first day of the first
month, the numbering took place a month after. The
sockets, chapters and filaments may have been made
just before. They may perfectly well have given each
man his money, and the actual numbering been made
six weeks afterwards to verify it, and that number **be**
given as the ascertained one, even if some few had
attained the age of twenty in the short interval. The
command to give the half shekel is given in chapter **30.**
But this was by no means all the silver, for many had
offered willingly, but it was typically important that **it**
should be understood that that on which the tabernacle

of witness was founded was redemption, and what
separated the service of God from the world was redemption. Hence the sockets of the boards of the
tabernacle and the hooks and chapiters on which the
hangings of the court were fixed were of this silver.—
The actual numbering took place when the tabernacle
was set up to verify the number redeemed, which had its
own importance. If some shekels more were given it
was of no consequence whatever to notice them, as the
direction for their use was given already. Some few
might have died who had given their half shekel, some
few reached twenty, but the sum, when numbered, is
taken as the sum applied to the service. We know that
the population in the wilderness was as nearly stationary
as possible.

The next difficulty is how they got tents, on leaving
Egypt, and carried them. I might fairly say I do not know.
Some may have been badly off for want of them, have made
them on the journey, and while staying at Sinai for a
year. As to carrying them, nothing is said; they had
asses doubtless, perhaps camels, as well as oxen. The
history says nothing about it. To say they could not
have them is absurd. Very likely they were at first greatly in want of them. All this is to the last degree idle: it
is not the object of the history to give these details. Dr.
C. then takes a very difficult Hebrew word to prove that
if it means "armed," there are difficulties in knowing
how they got arms, or how they were afraid of Pharaoh
if they had. It is really tedious to go through such ab-
surdities. The word probably signifies that they went
out "in array,"—not as poor hunted runaways: for God
took them out with a high hand. "By strength of hand
the Lord brought us out of Egypt." But it does not by
any means follow, if their faith were not lively, that they
would not be alarmed when attacked by trained soldiers.
It is said in this same 13th chapter: God did not take

them the short way lest the people should repent when they saw war, and return to Egypt. And they were so disposed. God suffered their faith to be tried for a moment, and they did repent when they saw war; only now it was but to make His deliverance the more conspicuous. Nor, where faith was not in exercise, was it very wonderful. Accustomed to be slaves, with all their women and children and cattle, the way of escape barred, no practice in war or even in any common military arrangements, they were in face of the most experienced warriors on earth, with chariots and cavalry;—themselves a great mixed multitude. When Dr. C says " a body of 600,000 warriors," he says what is false. They were not warriors. They were of an age fit for war, even if that were true of them; but they were poor brickmakers, though now roused by God's intervention to leave the house of bondage.

The next objection as to the passover, is founded on misstatement and carelessness. Dr. C. insists it was impossible to notify it, and have all ready in time. He tells us the first notice of any such feast to be kept is given in this very chapter, where we find it written, verse 12. " I will pass through the land of Egypt *this night.*" Hence he argues it was impossible to have all Israel ready, and insists on *this night* and the use of the Hebrew word hazeh. But zeh has not this kind of exactitude always. At any rate the chapter shews distinctly the falseness of the conclusion Dr. C. has drawn from it. The directions had been given at the beginning of the month, and the lamb had to be kept up three days; " This month shall be unto you the beginning of months, it shall be the first month of the year to you. Speak ye unto all the congregation of Israel, saying: on the tenth day of this month they shall take to them every man a lamb, . . . and ye shall keep it up until the fourteenth day of the same

nonth." Dr. C. says this cannot mean that they had
1otice several days beforehand, because it says, I will
)ass through the land of Egypt this night. This is very
)ad indeed. Moses is told to notify to all the people to
ake a lamb the tenth, and to keep it to the fourteenth, and
his we are told cannot mean that they got notice before-
1and, because the chapter says "this night," when it
:omes to killing and eating it. And what can it mean
:lse ? If the lamb was not kept up from the tenth to the
'ourteenth, the ordinance was not kept at all. All this
)bjection does, is to disclose the will of the objector.
No doubt the momentous ordinance itself is what occu-
)ies the inspired writer, but the beginning of the chapter
'ully suffices to shew that the objection drawn from want
)f time and notice, is as perverse as it is unfounded.
The rest of the article does not deserve notice. In the
first place kids would do, so that there was no danger of
all the male lambs perishing. As to notice to start, they
ate it, loins girded, and staff in hand, ready to go, and
were prepared long before to be on the move, to sacrifice
in the wilderness. Nor is there a word to shew there
was any sudden notice ; or that their move was caused
by the urging of the Egyptians.

Dr. C. thinks that his own confusion, in fright from a
false alarm, proves that there must have been hopeless
confusion in Israel. But they had for a length of time been
demanding to move with all their flocks, and were now
loins girt and staff in hand, so that we cannot doubt a
moment that all was prepared and arranged. There is
no hint of an order to start communicated suddenly.
The Egyptians were urgent on them to go. They had
already borrowed jewels from the Egyptians in antici-
pation of going. The whole theory of Dr. C. is simply
inattention to the scriptural account. Because that
account dwells chiefly on the great facts which have
a moral import he concludes there were none else even

when they are positively stated, and makes statements
moreover, and statements upon which all his argument
depends, which are not in the passage, or actually contradict it. I may add that I do not even admit that the
600,000 were only men in the prime of age; they were
all above twenty—twenty and above, that were men,
besides children. This would make a considerable
difference in the numbers.

As to how the herds were fed in the desert, it is certain
they chose their encampment where there were springs.
At Sinai God gave them water out of a rock. I may
add that Dr. C. speaks of Mount Serbal as Sinai, which is
more than doubtful, or confounds two opinions, applying
statements as to one incorrectly to the other, ignorant that
there was any difference; which, as to the character of
the place of encampment, is important. Lipsius thought
Serbal was Sinai, but more exact research has made it
pretty clear it was not, and shewn where Israel encamped.
The attempt to say, as Dr. C. says, that the wandering
in the desert is not a necessary preliminary to all the
history of Israel, is too barefaced, does too much violence
to the common sense of every man who has read scripture
to call for an answer. Movements of whole nations in
the deserts of Upper Asia have been frequent when there
was not the miraculous interposition of God to give
water, which is stated in the history of Israel. Israel
stayed mainly in the north of the desert on the borders
of Mount Seir and the land of Canaan, where there were
wells and pasture. Though what is related in detail is
what happened at Sinai at the beginning, and at the close.
When Dr. C. says the Scripture story says not a word
about this long sojourn near Mount Seir and the Red Sea
he makes a blunder with his usual carelessness. The
Israelites got through the desert of El Tyh* (which is not

*El Tyh is a modern name (the wandering) for the desert district lying
north of Sinai.

the desert of Sinai as Dr. C. says) by a rapid and short journey to the desert of Paran and Kadesh Barnea close to Canaan. There they were called on to go up the mountain of the Amorites and take possession of the land. Instead of this they sent the spies, the Lord giving His sanction to it, but at their desire. Their faith failed and they would not go up, and were condemned to wander the forty years, till the men, save Joshua and Caleb, died.

It was on their refusal to go up that they turned and went to the Red Sea (Numbers xiv. 25), and then it was they compassed Mount Seir (Deut. i. 40), and were on the border of countries affording supplies. In one place where they had no water they were given it again miraculously, went down finally outside the Wady Akaba to the Red Sea, returned to Mount Hor for Aaron's death, and then, at last, down to the Red Sea again, going up the eastern side of the mountains of Seir to Moab and Jordan. The statement of Dr. C. is merely the result of carelessness in searching Scripture. The detail of these long years we have not; but we have of a stay of a year in Sinai, where water was given miraculously, a short journey across El Tyh, the Lord himself leading them, their arrival at the borders of the land, and their journeying about Mount Seir and to the Red Sea, water being given them miraculously when it failed. Let me remark how beautifully at the moment they were sent back from the land through their unbelief (Numb. xiv.) God gives direc-tions what to do in the land, shewing His promise and purpose as sure as His Word and nature, in spite of man's folly and failure.—Numb. xv. The only account we have of the stations between their reaching the borders of the land in the second year, and their reaching Jordan, is in Num. xxxiii., and the localities at which they stopped during this interval of time are unknown till we come to Moseroth. Thence their journey is clear to the Red

Sea, back to Hor, back to the Red Sea, and round Seir to
Edom. (Comp. Numb. xxi. and Deut. x.) But we know
that from Kadesh to Zered was thirty-eight years, so that
they reached Kadesh in the second year before the end
of it, probably a good while before, because the wars
against the Amorites and Og were after Zered and before
Jordan. Now they did not leave Sinai till the end of the
second month of the second year. They abode in Kadesh
many days, certainly more than forty, so that we are sure
that the journey from Sinai to the borders of Canaan was
very short indeed. They were there on the edge of
cultivated land. God turned them back, but they never
left the neighbourhood of Canaan, Seir, and the Red Sea.
And He who turned them back took care of them, giving
them water at Meribah miraculously when needed. Of
all this Dr. C. is ignorant, telling us Scripture says nothing about it,—not having examined that which he is
pretending to prove unhistorical. This is true that the
Lord gives us those parts of the journey in detail which
have a moral bearing, and not how the cattle were provided for. But the book is all false if it be not historical.
We have the name of each place where they stopped during
the whole forty years. This must be history or forgery.
I have noticed elsewhere that the statement in Deut. x.
seems to contradict the list in Numbers but becomes the
strongest proof of the historical character of the book
when closely examined, because we find, by careful
comparison of facts and passages, that they traversed the
same ground twice from Hor to the Red Sea, from the Red
Sea to Hor, and then back to the Red Sea and east of Edom.
But men do not make these apparent contradictions,
solved by collateral facts and shewn to be unconsciously
true, save in relating real history, which, as they know
the facts, they have no need to combine and arrange.

Dr. C. makes difficulties as to there being wild beasts
in Canaan with so large a population. His objections

are futile. What is the population of India? how dense
is well known, yet tigers and wild beasts abound.
Modern European populations are no rule at all, nor
even Port Natal, because they settled more in Canaan in
towns and villages. Counting in the Canaanites besides
Israel is only another instance of Dr. C's. carelessness,
for the supposition made is their total immediate destruction. My own conviction is that the number of Israelites
is greatly exaggerated. The 600,000 are all males not
children, all the grown men.

The whole of the reasoning in the next chapter to
prove the first-born more numerous than is stated seems
to me an undoubted mistake. I cannot doubt that·
those only, and the same in Egypt, who were still
members of their father's families are counted. The
captive in the dungeon and Pharaoh himself may have
been first-born, but it is not supposed, as in question,
that they should die. It was the house. " There was
not a house where there was not one dead." In each
family which was together the first-born was taken. I
do not believe that a first-born father and his first-born son
were both taken or numbered. The first-born children of
child-bearing mothers were counted. The first-born of
existing families at the time of the numbering. It clearly,
I apprehend, did not include old men and grandfathers
whose fathers were dead, or even heads of families married
out, but first-born of living mothers whose families were
with them. Hence counted from a month old. Those
below were yet unclean. Remark here that the question
must have presented itself to the mind of the writer. It is
a proof that *it is* historical that an *evident* difficulty is left
unsolved. A forger does not put an evident difficulty in his
account. Here we have an apparent and evident difficulty.
The number of grown men is in the previous chapter. No
explanation given. Why? Because the writer is stating
facts, not inventing a story, and therefore states the fact

without noticing the difficulty. For myself, I can only say, when I never thought of a question in it, I never took the statement as to Egypt or Israel as referring to other than families at home, unmarried members of households. Indeed, in this particular case, it may be questioned whether it was not those only born after the destruction of the first-born Egyptians to whom the ordinance here referred to was given. God says he sanctified then to Himself all the first-born. It would, perhaps, suppose an unusual number in their first year of liberation, which would be nothing extraordinary. However, on this I do not insist, as those under a month must be subtracted, who, in this case, might be numerous. " All the males," does not refer to all of all ages, but all the males as contrasted with females. Indeed, in verse 43, it is rather implied that all were not : ". and all the first-born males by the number of names, from a month old and upwards of those that were numbered of them, were 22,273." But neither do I insist on this, as the Hebrew may, I apprehend, be taken as " in their numbering " the same as " in number."

As to the question of the increase of population during the sojourn of Israel in Egypt it has been discussed and rediscussed a hundred times, and it must require overweening self-confidence in Dr. C. to bring it forward as he does as an *argumentum crucis*. He says the doubts he has " raised will be confirmed into a certain conviction, by its appearing plainly from the data of the Pentateuch that there could not have been any such population itself to come out of Egypt," p. 148. I suppose he must be ignorant of what has been said of it; if not, such language is simply overweening impertinence to men far better versed in such inquiries than himself. If the Israelites doubled in fifteen years, they would have been 1,146,880 in two hundred and fiften years ; in two hundred and thirty years 2,293,760. But the statement of Scripture is, that

" the children of Israel were fruitful and increased abun-
dautly, and multiplied, and waxed exceeding mighty,
and the land was filled with them ;" and the new king
said, " Behold, the people of the children of Israel are
more and mightier than we," . . . and they perse-
cuted them. Very probably they were all removed to
Goshen, giving rise to Manetho's story of Avaris. " But
the more they afflicted them the more they multiplied and
grew," so that their increase was not such as makes any
difficulty. In England the increase in ten years was more
than 23 per cent., where town and manufacturing habits
largely impede, so that 35 per cent. in fifteen years is
reached in the actual state of England. So that doubling
in the circumstances of Israel, with extraordinary bless-
ing in this respect, was nothing incredible, though we
have no proof of their numbers more than the 600,000
males above twenty, and no proof that the majority of
women were not Egyptians or other strangers. If this
fact be taken into account, the increase presents no kind
of difficulty. But the duration of the sojourn is a very
obscure point : Josephus gives it both as two hundred
and fifteen and as four hundred and thirty. The reader
may see Clinton Fynes' investigation of the point, if he
have access to it. He reckons two hundred and fifteen
years, taking the shorter or Hebrew chronology. Many
able chronologists doubt of this, as Hales. At first sight
Gal iii. 17 seems to decide the question, but when examined it does not, I think, necessarily do so. The apostle
takes the time of promise as a general fact. To Abraham
were the promises made and to his seed. Now the confirmation to the seed does not come in for some forty
years after the promise. It is of this confirmation the
apostle speaks, if we take the letter of what he says. But
his object was not the date, save as showing the law
coming long after the promise. He refers to Ex. xii. 40,
which was sufficient for him, and is ambiguous. He

may refer to patriarchal times as those of promise, and
take the Egyptian state as four hundred and thirty years.
The length of the sojourn in Egypt is an unsettled question.

As to the Chronicles, it is, I judge, a blunder of Dr.
C.'s, which I should not think much of, were not his book
solely founded on affected accuracy of detail. 1 Chron.
vii. 20, presents difficulties. This is always hopeful
ground for infidels. What is difficult to understand they
can more easily turn to their own purpose, for others
have not a positive answer ready. If we follow the
statement simply, however, there is no great difficulty.
The Chronicles, besides giving the history of Judah,
not Israel, and especially of David's family, gather up
all the fragments possible of ancient history and genealogy for the return of Israel from Babylon. Take the
passage thus—" The sons of Ephraim Shuthelah :" his
genealogy is followed down to a second Shuthelah, and
there stops. Then the passage speaks of two other sons
of Ephraim, Ezer and Elead, who made a raid against
Gath, and were killed; and then follows another son of
Ephraim, which is quite natural, and *his* genealogy is
given. His daughter Sherah is simply a descendant of
his. Ammihud was fifth from Ephraim.

The objection to the numbers of the Danites and Levites,
that of the former being large, though Dan had only one
son, which, to an unpractised eye, may seem to present the
greatest difficulty, is founded on want of attention to the
reckonings of scripture; as if in every case those mentioned
are all. The very comparison with Chronicles which Dr.
C. institutes ought to have taught him it was not so; for
there are persons mentioned there who are not in Exodus. The genealogies are given as far as needed to make
out the moral history according to God's government of
Israel, but no farther. Any number may be left out, even
generations may, provided what is needed is given.—

Next, generations are taken by Dr. C. as if they were
the same then as now. They lived one hundred and thirty
or one hundred and forty years, and their families were
often proportionate, and here God interfered expressly to
multiply them. Thus if we had not Gen. xxv. all scripture would have led us to suppose that Ishmael and
Isaac were all the sons Abraham had. Here we see he
had six sons more when he was quite an old man, of
whom nations sprung. Here for other purposes it was
important to notice it. In other cases it was not. Next
the assumption that Israel remained only two hundred
and fifteen years in Egypt is a questionable one.

The number of the generation following the twelve pa-
triarchs is no way decided. To begin the computation
one really ought to take at any rate one hundred and
thirty-nine, not seventy; that is, take the females in. So
the children of Dinah and Serah do not appear at all.
The fact of a number of children in one generation says
nothing as to the result. Benjamin had many; Reuben
had many. Neither were large tribes. Does Dr. C. suppose that a forger would have been insensible to this if
he had been inventing. It is the strongest possible proof
that the account is historical, drawn from facts, for no one
would have laid himself open to the objection. There
was no need whatever, but that the facts were so, to lend
a handle to objectors. It was un atural if it were not
true. Dr. C. states that Moses' children were only two.
I doubt it much. They were only two by Zipporah, but
he had married also an Ethiopian woman. It did not
concern the scripture history to say anything of children
by her. We see from the genealogies that families were
reckoned all under one head if they were not numerous
so as to make a distinct family—1st Chron. xxiii. 10, 11—
or might come in as two when properly the head should
have been but one, as Ephraim and Manasseh. If Joseph
had had a dozen sons afterwards they would not have

c

formed distinct families—Gen. xlviii. 6. They would
have merged in the tribes of Ephraim and Manasseh.*

All these considerations which lie at the basis of the
whole system are ignored by Dr. C. We have an instance
how much the names are taken merely to represent families, and how many may be left out, in the very case Dr.
C. mentions, who in his usual careless and superficial
way does not notice or perceive it, being simply bent on
his own object. " The Amramites, he tells us, numbered
as Levites in the fourth (Eliezer's) generation were, as
above, only two, namely, the two sons of Moses,—the sons
of Aaron being reckoned as Priests. Hence the rest of the
Kohathites of this generation must have been made up of
the descendants of Ishar and Uzziel," p. 169-170. This
is because Ishar and Uzziel are mentioned—Exodus. vi.
21, 22. But this is simply that there was some special
reason for mentioning them. Kohath had another son,
Hebron, who may have had for ought we know ten times
as many. In a word those are noticed in the genealogies
as to whom some special motive existed, others not.
Dr. C. has not even found it out. All his calculation here
is based, to say nothing of its general fallacy, upon his
not noticing what was before his eyes in the text. But
this fact, with a thousand other similar ones, involves a
principle which makes the ground of all his calculations
fundamentally false. Let the reader note this case, as it
may clear his mind as to these statements of families.
A genealogical succession is given, and only two sons
out of four mentioned. One, it so happens, we can
supply as far as it goes, because Moses and Aaron came
from that stock,—the absence of the other we cannot ac-

* As to Dan, if the absence of others of the tribe not yet formed hin-
dered the application of the rule laid down in the case of Zelophehad's
daughters, the fact that he had only one son may have been removed in
a few generations. Hushim may have had as many as Jair who had thirty
sons who rode on thirty asses colts.

coun t for. In this case we are sure of it, because he is
mentioned a few verses before. Now it is just as possible, very likely indeed, that Amram may have had a host
of sons besides Moses and Aaron who are mentioned
because of their importance. The names are given more
to show from whom people are descended who are known,
than to tell all the descendents. All this Dr. C. has over-
looked, and simply made mathematical calculations as
if all were given.—His whole system is false.

Dr. C.'s computations are merely neglect of all the
principles of scriptural genealogics. Besides, I repeat,
the numbers given are such as prove they are not fabri-
cated; and the paucity of Levites, and the numbers of Dan
prove that the statements are drawn from history and
facts, as the whole tenor of the statements bear on the
face of them, and are such as no man on earth would
have invented. Dr. C. says:—It is incredible the Levites should not have increased more during the sojourn
in the wilderness. The fact that Eliezer did not die proves
nothing as to the Levites not coming under the judgment
which fell on Israel, for their murmerings when the spies
returned; God was pleased to keep Israel at the same
level in the wilderness. As to numbers that is clear.
The Levites were no exception. God may have used
providential means for this, the privations of the wilderness, which affected the Levites as well as the rest. But
there is no motive for thinking they were exempt from
the judgment. But the truth is the great change in
relative numbers in the tribes shews all the reasoning as
to the small increase of the Levites, utterly valueless.
Population may increase or decrease at such a rate, but
that says nothing whatever for particular families. One
increases, another becomes extinct. Thus Manasseh
rose from 32,200 to 52,700. Ephraim had sunk from
40,500 to 32,500. Benjamin increased from 35,410 to
45,600. Dan was stationary. Asher had increased

fror.. 41,500 to 53,400. Judah had remained pretty stationary. Issachar largely increased. Simeon had fallen from fifty-nine thousand to twenty-two. Thus the particular degree of the increase of the Levites, on which Dr. C. has bestowed so much labour, is of no import whatever. All Dr. C.'s remarks indicate a singular in-attention to facts.

As regards the small number of Priests making it impossible they could fulfil their services; unless in the case of the offering of birds, it is a mistake to think the priest had anything to do save to receive the blood, and arrange a burnt-offering on the altar. All the operations of slaying, flaying, cutting up, were done by the offerer. But let it be remembered we are speaking of history. The doctrinal import, (which is their real value) of the directions for the sacrifices, is most precious as these are known types of the sacrifice of Christ. No part of Scripture is more important. This of course is lost on Dr. C. Now as to *history*, we have no proof that a single offering was brought all the time they were in the wilderness. Burnt-offerings were always voluntary, and, in the state of Israel, it is just as likely they never troubled their heads about it; for they sinned without compunction, and certainly had never circumcised their children, so that really they had no right to offer any sacrifice. That they did not offer a peace offering is certain, for they murmured for meat, complaining of the manna, and got the quails in chastisement; at any rate on the second occasion. Save Miriam we do not hear of any one having the leprosy. There is no evidence of any historical difficulty what-ever, but the contrary. Indeed, Amos. v. 25, complains that they did not offer sacrifice to Jehovah, but took Moloch and Chiun for their Gods. History, therefore, has nothing to do with the matter; the instruction as to priests and sacrifices, is doctrinal, *not* historic. The details of Dr. C.'s reasonings are as trifling as usual.

As Scripture speaks often of doves in the wilderness, he assures us the psalmist was hardly thinking of the terrible deserts of Sinai—of which he knows nothing. Was ever more egregious trifling?

As regards the Passover, Dr. C. says it was impossible the priests could suffice to kill the passover, and sprinkle the blood. If, as it is evident they naturally would, they kept it as they had in Egypt, every house killed the lamb for itself. The whole difficulty is a soap bubble, proving only Dr. C.'s will and foolishness. If Dr. C. had given himself the trouble of reading, 2 Chron. xxx., which he quotes, he would have seen that the Levites (verse 17) killed the passover, because many of the people had not sanctified themselves, and they did so only for those who were not clean. It rather appears that it was the blood of the burnt-offering which the priests sprinkled then. At any rate this, and Josiah's passover, when the priest did sprinkle the blood of the paschal lamb, were special exceptional cases, and there were plenty of priests and Levites attending in their places. As far as the New Testament goes it would seem each prepared it for himself. It is really disgraceful for a person in Dr. C.'s position, or for any one, to make a formal attack on a Book he has professed to believe in, on grounds so futile and with a carelessness which proves no honest research for himself, but that his will was father to his thought. He has at any rate proved himself, logarithims and all, to be an equally incompetent and pretentious man. Probably, those, by whom nine years ago, he assures us, he was not thought unworthy of the position which he holds, supposed that, in declaring he believed in all the canonical Scriptures, he said the truth. Just think of a man taking the battle of Waterloo (and on the side of the victorious army, well knowing, as every one does, it is in pursuit most are slain,) as a test of the numbers of Asiatic armies, as to which a child, who has read

Rollin•' History of Greece or Persia, knows the difference.

Dr. C. complains of the destructive Razzia against Midian. Midian had been the means of corrupting Israel, and leading them to idolatry, so as to lead to 25,000 Israelites falling in the pestilence God sent; and that by the inexpressible wickedness of Balaam, who, when he could not curse Israel, recommended Balak to lead them into sin, and then God could not bless them. For this they were punished, and, as a settled nation there, destroyed. Dr. C. congratulates himself that he is not called on to believe it. But thus he must give up the whole Old Testament for his own notions; he must give up God's judging the world. God sent Abraham's seed down into Egypt because the iniquity of the Amorites was not yet full. The whole history is a history of the judicial extermination of these races for their wickedness. It is a question not of history, but of the whole ways and dealings of God in judgment. He will find it in the Psalms; he will find it in Revelations. God presents Himself as a moral governor, and in this special case used human instruments to carry out His judgments, as He did afterwards against Israel, as He had warned them by the prophets. The whole establishment of Israel was founded on the principle rejected by Dr. Colenso: all God's judgments are. Dr. C. does not like to believe in judgment. Be it so. But that is no way of judging of history. As to God's revelation of Himself, it is objected that the Old Testament character of God cannot be that of the true God. He did not reveal Himself in Judaism. He gave laws, promises, but He dwelt in thick darkness—was avowedly hid behind the veil. The way into the holiest was not made manifest. He was patient in goodness and grace, but the system was one of public moral government. The sins of the fathers could be visited on their children, as we see still in providential government. There was a code of national laws, of which Christ could say, " Moses for the hardness of your hearts gave you this commandment." In the national laws he did not set aside slavery. The law made nothing perfect. He took, as a people in the world, the people where they were ; put checks on will, softened in many respects the manners of the age by His authority, and what was an immense point, suffered nothing to be done without it— an immense point, because arbitrary will was arrested. But all this was not bringing souls to God, nor revealing God as he is to souls. He is light and love. He has been revealed in Christ, a revelation Dr. C., it appears, is content to give up. He is so wise, so competent to know God, and judge of what He ought to be, that he can give up all revelation of Him ; and yet is ignorant of the first principles of the revelation he is giving up, and publishes an empty book, if ever there was one, to prove it,—assuming, as his statements are conclusive, Moses and all the prophets are ignoramuses, Christ knows no better than the Rabbis, but Dr. C., of course, does. Christ attaches His sanction to the whole of the Old Testament, as having the authority of God. Now this does not merely affirm inspiration : it is the blessed Lord putting His seal to God's having been justly represented there *as thus revealed.* Dr. C. thinks differently ; he would not have such a God—is relieved in thinking it is not true. Christ felt no need of such relief. What shall we think of one who holds the nominal place of bishop of the Christian Church, who counts himself the moral supe- rior of the Lord ? Who else will think so ? Think of the vanity and character of the man who could. Did ever a man degrade himself to the same degree ! For Christ did not see any thing moral to make Him call in question its being a revelation of God. Dr. C. does. Christ could see that there were national laws given, as suited to the hardness of their hearts. That Dr. Colenso does not see.

He is as ignorant of the relationship of the Gospel to the
law as a national code, as he is presumptuous and ill-
founded in judging the law and slighting the Gospel.
For every man of sense the book will do good.

But I will complete the question of detail as to the
Midianites. Numb. xxxi.; Comp. xxi. 1, and xxxiii. 33–
40. The objection is, that time is not allowed for the destruction and other events before Moses addressed the
people, Deut. i. 3. I have, as will be seen, no objection
to the result at which Dr. C. arrives ; but I will show the
levity of the proofs, and then the excessive carelessness
of the author. There is no proof whatever of the time
employed in the destruction of Arad's cities. It is very
probable the prisoners alluded to had been taken thirty-
eight years before, when they would go up the mountain (Numb. xiv. 44, 45): they may or may not. Israel
then defeated now avenge themselves. Five days
may have very easily done the work. Further, it
appears rather to have been carried into effect during
the mourning for Aaron, for they left Mount Hor afterwards, Numbers xxviii. 41. Next we are told that
there was a fortnight for the serpents and healing,
and *then* a month of journeyings. This is the usual inattention to the facts. They moved on from one station to
another, and murmured because of the way, and the
serpents were sent *while on the journey.* They had
made four encampments of this journey, before the serpents were sent ; this is certain, by comparing Numb. xxi.
10 and xxxiii. 41-43. Thus the three months and-a-half
become perhaps a month and a-half or two months.
Sihon was defeated. It may have been in a day and
the country fell to Israel. They marched thence up north,
and Og came out with all his people and was defeated.
For all this there may have been a month possibly more.
Thus three months at the outside would have *sufficed* for
what Dr. C. takes six months for. Let it be three and a

half. This much is certain that in the point where Dr. C. is precise, tne serpents and supposed subsequent journey, he is precisely wrong by not consulting the text. Dr. C. then for the remaining facts gives " March forward to the plains of Moab." March forward from where? They were in Moab, the expeditions had started thence. But they were by Arnon the border of Moab. They made then very short stages. They might move their head-quarters, but they were in Moab, only they moved into the plain from Mount Abarim. Balak was alarmed and sent for Balaam. This may have taken a week. We have thus some four months gone. Here Israel fell into sin with Moab, and thereupon Israel attacks the Midian-ites by divine command. My statements leave two months for this. I should be quite disposed to say with Dr. C., six weeks perhaps, and probably four, was ample so as to allow a month more for the previous marches and wars. No one can pretend to say how much each took; there was time enough for all. But this is not even necessary, though it sufficed to shew the arbitra-ness and even error of Dr. C.'s calculations. More was spent in some parts; in others the text contradicts him. But what is curious enough is that Dr. Colenso has made the passages he holds to be irreconcilable, so as to prove they are unhistoric, *exactly coincide* by his computation, and has not found it out. Moses' address in Deut. i. 3, is after defeating Sihon and Og, as it is expressly stated, verse 4. Dr. C. says " Thus, then, from the first day of the fifth month, in which Aaron died, to the completion of the conquest of Og, king of Basham, we cannot reckon less together than six months . . . and are thus brought down to the first day of the eleventh month, the very day on which Moses is stated to have addressed the people in the plains of Moab, Deut. i. 3 " Just so, accordingly Deut. i. 4, states that it was after he had slain Og, that he made the address. Dr. C. has managed to make a

D

blunder in his proofs, but has tumbled by mistake, into
proving exactly historic what he attacks, and this is to
set aside the Bible by unquestionable facts.

On the quotations from Cicero and the Hindoo author
celebrating Ram, I have spoken, and add no more here.
A more pretentious and futile attempt to set aside the
revelation of God, it never came to my lot to examine.

It may be well just to add that the quotation from
' types of mankind' which Dr. Colenso quotes, as he
says, with entire sympathy, is from one of two works
by Messrs. Gliddon and Nott to prove that there are
several races of mankind, as there are of animals, and
following the analogy of the forms of these last, according
to a theory of Agassiz, the object being to prove that the
negroes are a distinct race, and formed and destined to
be fit for slavery. I can hardly think that if he was so
zealous with the Zulu for the honour of the true God as
to condemn the Pentateuch because it recognized slavery
in Israel, that he can have read the book. It is very
superficial, is wrong according to the best authorities as
to America, particularly South America, and contradicts
itself as to Africa. His only argument, to which he
(Mr. Gliddon) constantly recurs, being the presence of
negro figures on the Egyptian monuments, of which,
with Lipsius and others, he exaggerates the antiquity
in a way which the monuments themselves clearly prove
to be false, inasmuch as kings given as successive are
proved by the monuments to be contemporary, as many
as eight at a time. Mr. Gliddon was Consul General of
the United States in Egypt. I quite admit Dr. C. does
not quote the book in what it says of negroes, but the
argument which meets his entire sympathy is used to
get rid of the 'prejudice' which believes with Paul that
' God has made of one blood all nations of men for to
dwell on all the face of the earth,' in order to justify the
reducing the blacks to slavery as a distinct race.

ND - #0072 - 290922 - C0 - 229/152/3 - PB - 9780259505358 - Gloss Lamination